Layers

D'Shan Berry

/ BookLeaf
Publishing

India | USA | UK

Made with ❤ on the BookLeaf Publishing Platform

www.bookleafpub.in

www.bookleafpub.com

Dedication

To the P.A.W.S. of Roswell, NM

Thanks for all your support and encouragement!
Y'all have enriched my life in so many ways.
Love y'all!

Preface

Acknowledgements

Special Thanks

Marie Manning
and
Helen Walters

For pushing me to finish this book.

The Dash

A life is born, then starts the dash,
The hyphen in between
That day and the final morrow
On which a life is gleaned.

For some, the dash is decades long,
For others the same date
Bookends the dash, tragically short,
A sad, too common fate.

We know not what our dash will hold
Until we reach its end.
May yours hold life well lived and years
With family and friends.

Old Scars

Self-injury awareness month,
A cause dear to my heart,
Necessitates my openness
And willingness to start

A dialogue about the pain
I covered up so long,
And how I learned to cope with it
By poems and with songs.

I imploded after trauma,
Suffering all alone;
My feelings buried deep inside
But yearning to be known.

Not wanting to hurt other folks,
I turned my wrath on me.
I felt I'd earned it, anyway,
Instead of being free.

The guilt and shame kept me silent
And wholeness farther away.
Only by sharing my stories,
Has healing come to stay.

The cost to tell my story—now
Ransom for another.
By speaking up, light pierces dark
And we help each other.

Strength

Where lies the good in having strength,
Without lifting others?
When we can bear more of the weight,
We should help our brothers.

For we are all one family;
We're more alike than not.
We need to learn to love again;
Each other's all we've got.

Hurt People

They say, "Hurt people, hurt people,"
But those who hurt can heal.
Pain can also bring empathy
Not otherwise revealed.

Who best to help with suffering
Than those who've walked it's roads?
Who understand the weariness,
Who've carried heavy loads?

So, sometimes, hurt means lashing out,
But, like compost piles,
Hurts can foster growth and new life
From our many trials.

So, be the rule's exception
And heal instead of hurt.
Let compassion transform your life;
Your tenderness, exert.

Shifting Tides

The distant, lunar gravity
Pushes and pulls the tide;
Engulfing then exposing land
Across the oceans wide.

So, too, the gravity of grief
Affects and changes our hearts;
Surges of sorrow and suff'ring
Rising, like high tide starts.

Then, the low tide of loneliness
Lays your tender heart bare
Revealing the depths of your love,
How much you'll always care.

But, if we can learn to ride the waves
Between tides low and high,
Then our grief won't pull us under
After we say goodbye.

Lament Upon Losing a Loved One

Soul-splitting pain, without relent;
So many tears I've cried.
You're the one whose heart has stopped,
But I feel like I've died;

At least, the version of myself
That I believed I knew
Has vanished in the wake of loss.
It's hard to know what's true.

And how is this all things working
Together for the good?!?
I feel lost and without answers.
I'd be numb, if I could.

And yet, I know, the only way
Out of this pain is through.
I must let myself feel sorrow
Before joy's born anew.

This Time

This time, I won't take forever
To open up to love;
To see in the mirror, at last,
A gift, sent from above.

Fitting in is not belonging,
So I'll give up trying.
Folding myself small for others
Left me almost dying,

But, like a phoenix birthed anew,
From the ashes, I'll rise;
Set free from darkness and shadows
To soar in sunlit skies.

Involuntary

So, sometimes, it felt good—
What a confusing cross to bear!
Affection and affliction, both,
From the exact same person shared.

My lonely spirit yearned
For warmth and attention and love.
Making me easy prey
For manipulations, thereof.

I know I had no choice
And my body just reacted,
But shame enveloped me,
While my self-worth, it subtracted.

But it was not my fault;
The shame not mine to bear, at all.
Speaking up—essential
For bringing down barrier walls.

I write this poem, now,
To break the stigma all apart,
To say you're not alone,
And that there's healing for your heart.

The Tree

The last leaf fell, but the tree stood
Waiting for spring to come;
Remembering other winters—
Oh, how the cold did numb!

But it had survived in the past;
Expected to, again.
The tree felt hope for the future,
Welling from deep within.

May you, also, retain that hope
Despite the winter's chill,
And may you ever bloom anew
In forests of goodwill.

Distillation

I set myself to steep in sun,
As though a jar of tea.
I soaked in warmth and light, and then,
Distilled the soul of me.

Tears

Like a prism, tears refract grief
Into glimmers of hope;
Our body's way to manage stress
And means to help us cope.

They wash away the "red" we've seen
After anger dissolves,
Or overflow from happiness.
They anoint and absolve.

So don't apologize for tears,
No matter what their cause.
Tears are not a sign of weakness.
They're blessings and not flaws.

Witness Bearing

This is the mission of my life—
bearing witness to pain,
To stop it from being unseen,
To hear its sad refrain.

Letting folks know they're not alone,
A simple act of care,
Can make a difference in their world,
Too often made unfair.

So, armed with two ears, I listen.
Listen to understand.
I've been given eyes to see it
'Cause I know it first-hand

But my suffering helps me see
The pain of those nearby.
I can help them feel less alone,
Though I can't answer, "Why?"

So, I'll go on, like a midwife—
Birthing validation,
Hoping to help heal my corner
Of God's great creation.

Masquerade

I have trouble trusting myself;
Too long, I've lived a lie.
I disowned who I was inside,
Forced myself to comply.

I felt survival depended
On masking the true me,
So I began to camouflage
Myself lest others see

The part of me that doesn't fit
The ideal form they hold.
Too shy to speak up, use my voice,
I did what I was told.

So, now I'm trying to relearn
My gut instincts again;
Rebelling from the lies I held
With poetry and pen.

Disorder

It seems like all I touch devolves to chaos,
  Spinning ever faster through the dark.
  Reeling, I can never catch my footing;
  Bewildered, I can never hit my mark.

Overloaded senses — side effect of grief,
Loss threatens to consume me, flesh and soul.
I pray each day to conquer my transgressions,
  To live a normal life, and be made whole.

Grief Letter

Dear mourning, I have long since sat
At your feet and studied.
The hard-earned wisdom you bestow—
Bandage for the bloodied.

If we let you, you can teach us
A deeper way to care;
As we grow around our grief,
And all our stories share.

Though your lessons may be trying,
Compassion is their fruit.
So, thanks for sharing your knowledge.
Your insights—all astute.

The Promise

"In this world, you will have trouble."
Christ said it would be so,
But He doesn't leave us lonely;
He never lets us go.

He is with us in the small things;
Won't vanish when they're large.
He can redirect our stories
If we put Him in charge.

So rest in this assurance, sweet—
You never walk alone.
No matter what the times befall,
Take heart, you are God's own.

Choices

"I am not what happened to me,
I am what I choose to become."
Carl Jung

I am not what happened to me,
But, rather, it's my choice;
What I become or want to do,
And how I use my voice.

I choose to focus on what's good
And not the pain I've known.
Now, sharing my story can help
Others feel less alone.

$ilence

The cost of remaining silent,
So difficult to bear,
Can emotionally bankrupt
Those soft enough to care.

The burden of keeping a secret,
A story yet untold,
Can wear a person down in life,
Age them before they're old.

Destiny

"So we beat on, boats against the current, borne back
ceaselessly into the past."
F. Scott Fitzgerald

Against the current, we beat on,
Borne back into the past.
We can't escape our foundations;
Our roots will hold us fast.

Regardless of how far we run,
Ourselves will meet us there.
Pretending to be someone else
Will work out almost ne'er.

Life Goes On

"In three words, I can sum up everything
I've learned about life:
it goes on."
Robert Frost

Life goes on despite our heartaches,
Despite the pain we feel,
And we can't pause happy moments
Like freeze-frame from a reel.

We cannot rush our grief, one bit,
And joy we cannot buy;
We only have one life to live
Before our time to die.

So, hold with loose hands your whole life,
Both the joy and sorrow,
And live each day like it's your last;
Hoping for tomorrow.

Marked

Scars like tattoos, each a story, each a badge of mettle,
Carved their way up both of her arms;
Old scores she had settled.

Having fought her inner demons,
Healing became her path;
Guiding others to their freedom
From hopelessness and wrath.

She planted her pain like a seed;
Grew to nourish others.
She tells her story to strangers—
New sisters and brothers.

So, life had left its marks on her,
Both real and in her heart,
But she has left her mark on it—
With Love, she did her part.

www.ingramcontent.com/pod-product-compliance
Lightning Source LLC
Chambersburg PA
CBHW051001030426
42339CB00007B/433